A Fire by the Sea

A Fire by the Sea

Alasdair Clayre

Compton Russell

Published in Great Britain by
Compton Russell Ltd., Compton
Chamberlayne, Salisbury, and
printed there by the
Compton Press Ltd.
ISBN 0 85955 004 4

ACKNOWLEDGEMENTS are due to Alan Ross Ltd. for
permission to reprint two of these poems which
appeared in *Poems from the London Magazine*.
Music for two of these poems is printed in
Adam and the Beasts: Songs by Alasdair Clayre,
Faber Music Ltd.

Contents

TWO EVENINGS

It was the time of dusk when lorry-drivers,
Running from Durham north to sea-fog nights,
Think about sleep, and switch on long-beamed lights
And the engine's monotonous drumming for a moment dies;
The time when half-light draws a fading gleam
From railway tracks, and ugly, unloved lovers,
Settling alone in trains to silent meals,
Hear a quickening of the wheels,
And see their faces trickling through the steam,
On carriage windows colder than their eyes.
I climbed upstairs about that time of day
Watching the last light set,
Then through an echoing flat could not forget
How evening felt before you were away.

SPRINGTIME SONG

The trees are bottles, just opened,
Foaming blossom spilling all over them
And I don't know where this is going to end.

Look down there : the water's clear,
And the light's jack-knifing out of the air,
And I don't know where this is going to end.

The trees are green like a watch at night,
Glowing in the criss-cross shadow and light
And I don't know where this is going to end.

And the clouds are gliding over the land
Like satisfied lovers hand in hand.
I don't know where this is going to end.

Two swans, wings stretched wide,
Are swinging round the water from side to side,
And I don't know where this is going to end.

This window fades out when the light shines through
My mind does that when I think about you,
And I don't know where this is going to end.

EASTER

Who would have thought that a year after
Her sudden beauty and his desire
He would at last have come to see
That time's truth, his one Easter;

That he would have pushed her away, wanting
Space to grow, to be free, whole;
And have grown up to his own hell
That her lost face would be constantly haunting.

She was like colours when day is passing
Early in spring, as soon seen
As gone; colours the vanished sun
With refracted beams makes doubly piercing.

AT A COCKTAIL PARTY

The restless husband with the drooping mouth
Looks round the cocktail party, picks out girls,
Stares, lights a cigarette and fidgets. By his side
His quiet-speaking wife stands, parchment sad
Extinguished lampshade that has trapped a moth.
Black hair sweeps up in coils
To crown her head, and hide the strands of grey
He has the air of hourly watching grow.
Are lovers nowadays
The ones who never reckon
That beauty has a timespan and then dies
Leaving the marriage-promise to be broken?
His eye has caught that sheath of crackling rayon;
A new girl idles up to sack the ruin.

REFUSAL TO PROPOSE

If I were gentle as a morning eye
Touching never less lightly
Whatever I loved than with the weight of a glance —
I could say: "Why don't we marry?" But instead
I pick a leaf and look away. I ought to say

"Your beauty stops my breath.
I cannot leave it as it is, free;
I want it to be registered as mine."
Or should I say; "Give me the slightest chance,
I'd pin you to a pillar like a vine.
Pluck you grape by grape
Tread out your smile and drink it for my wine."

CONTINUING

I speak so little. Let me try to say
How much you move me when I maunder in
And easing up to me you lay your thin
Hands in my hand, and kiss like the first day,

And when the moon has brought you near despair,
When tides have made your world a flux of red
And hiding in the shadow of your hair
You've flung your words like hatchets at my head.

GIRL'S SONG

It's summertime, and maybe that man loves me.
I feel the love I give him
Is how the world is going;
Through all this summer with him
I've seen his own love growing.
But when it comes to autumn
If he should change and leave me
How would I learn to live my life without him?

When autumn came, if he should change and leave me
I'd have a hundred lovers,
Not let my life be broken,
And all the lies he'd spoken
Whisper to the others.
But I'd be always crying
And if he turned to love me
How could we find our truth in so much lying?

GHOST IN THE STREET

The dark hair slanting down the face
To fringe one pale wide-open eye —
Venus adulterous on the flowers
Painted against a Pisan sky —

Crooks a slender wrist around
The soldier's neck, erect and vain,
Then drops to me, a pace behind
Her smile : "Deceiving you again."

JOURNEY

The jets tilt long swan necks up into
Dark. Below, necklaces of light —
Topaz, emerald — recede.
                                        Maps,
                                                voices,
To reassure that the safe pencil point will
Move us along the ruler to our destination.

Outside the thin glass, glare
Of lightning; clouds like diagrams of nerves
Lit.
    We buck;
                drop.
                        Suppose
Lightning strikes, or we two touch
Like cloud on cloud, shaking
The aimed plane : my life
With its purposes, hope, steady travelling
A row of chairs
Rocked in the lightning-fractured black air.

A FIRE BY THE SEA

Quarter to five : he scrapped the day's last box
And licked his dry lips of factory taste.
Sunlight was flooding low through broken boards
That blocked a window, flickering on the backs
Of workmen slouching coats on, brushing dust
From arms and sleeves. He heard the chink of birds
As each machine slowed down; then there was quiet.
With the tired crowd he jolted through the way out.

Sea-water glittered, and a hunch-backed combe
Closed round his motorbike echoing. By this road
He and the girl he used to love would ride
In summer to the sea. And now below
A broad bay opened where they used to swim
Or find the solitary rocks, and lie.
Between tall buttress-thrusts of purple cliff
The shore crooked in its sharp, remembered curve.

It shrank as he approached: wet bladder-wrack
Left by the waves in rotting swathes to dry
Had heaped it thick, muffling the breakers' arc.
He walked towards the water's edge again
And watched the sea. A clear last hour of day
Was wakening all the water's cypress green
To vivid jade, flaring on the foam's whiteness.
He listened, startled by the quiet's sweetness,

Then crunched thin shells. The sun sagged in a mound
Of clay-dark cloud; the waves' roar was the topple
Of hollow boxes across a floor, the shore
A dreary purple waste of factory rubble.
Flinging blunt stones into the crumpled sea
That slid at random with his tired mind
He watched the shadows cross from rock to rock
And bloom on damson headlands fade to black.

The darkening wind against his skin was cold.
He shivered, stooped, and heaped a fire of wood,
Gathering sticks ground rough as chicken's flesh
Or picked like bones by waves and smoothed to white,
Feeding them slowly as the night air cooled,
Watching their whiteness catch at the blaze, flush
And wizen crackling in a swirl of flame
Like the salt crackle of the bursting foam.

Now shafts of firelight lit the moving sea
Flaring along the unsteady crests of waves.
The darkness thickened, and he grew aware
Of how the wavering light-beams on the water
Had formed a pattern like the level grooves
That flute a deep-sea shell; and now he saw
This shell of light all round him where before
Had been rock chaos thrust back by the fire.

Now as he listened to the rollers' sound
It caught at the refrains in which he mourned:
Memories of the girl, the way his mind
Argued against her and her words of parting.
Each new wave's weight slumped crushed on stones and sand.
The sea-sound faded to his own heart beating.
A pale translucent firelight, gold like resin,
Spread as the air grew dark to the horizon.

Suddenly he got up and stretched a wrist,
Then stumbled up the shingle half awake.
The wheel-hubs of the bike were rimed with frost
Like cobweb in the dawn's encroaching grey.
Somewhere a first bird sang. He'd have to go
Now, if he was to sleep and eat and work.
The air was motionless and edged with dew.
He rode towards the first dark bronze of day.

PRISONER AWAITING EXECUTION

The watchtower moon now probes its ray more deep
Beneath the sea, and lights a bare-walled sky.
Within this brilliant prison, kept from sleep,
The human earth awaits her time to die.
Night engines, shunting guns with luxuries,
Arrange lost hopes of life in her tired brain;
White hunting owls, her dreams, float down through trees
And act the dropped shriek that will end her pain.
Only till morning, and her casual grace
Is lost like some arched movement of the sea;
Only a single hour, and her face
Is quite gone, like a madman's memory.
Under the bomber's moon she wakes to pray
For time, to let the execution stay.

PHILOSOPHER DRINKING WINE

The oboes on the terrace held a chord
And died away to silence. Clitheroe poured —
Bored — still more brandy for the moon-faced priest;
The moon hung rusty in the clouded east.
Oboe and harpsichord, more slow and high,
Began the adagio. "Eighteen children die
For want of food in India at each chord,"
Thought Clitheroe, with precision, as he poured.

PHILOSOPHER WALKING

"Terrified by the machinery at work
Inside my head, I dread one wasted hour.
Without first calculating that the air
Will do me good, I scarcely dare to walk.
Still with my freedom for the next day perfect
The object of my life's work is to die
Reckoning with satisfaction that each day
Has been employed to yield the maximum profit.
Those fifteen minutes spent in merely looking
Can only pass without self-racking anger
If they supplied the pause that I was lacking
For better work, or stilled some lonely hunger
That might wreck all this kept-back life at once
In some one love that I could not renounce."

PHILOSOPHER URGENT

My words have no general application
  Come out into the sun
Serious perplexities will survive my proposal
  Walk to the top of the hill
I do not imply universalisability
  Lie down under this tree.

MELANIE KLEIN'S THEORY

Black cypress-shadow weaves
Over the yellow globes
And seaweed-heavy leaves
Of midday grapefruit groves;
A child curls his wet tongue
Seeing such sweetness hang,
Tastes, then twists his dry-wrung
Mouth at the bitter tang,

And spits away this strange
Sweet lemon, sour orange;

But grows to reconcile
Sourer and sweeter pole,
And in a little while
Desires this new-found whole
More than the easy taste
That pleased his palate first,
And what he spat in haste
Comes to long for in thirst.

CARMARTHENSHIRE

Fy lloer â'i gwallt fal lliw'r gwin,
A'i phryd fal ffrwd y felin.

APRIL

The trees go suddenly brilliant green
As wind unsettles arpeggios of washing —
Stave for a thrush to sing
Over a bass of lorry engines.
Traffic rolls glittering on
And hard-edged shadow on cat-blue roof-tops
Jumps down the front of shops
Onto awnings striped white and crimson.
Colours are sun-puppets — they dangle
On cords the clouds pull;
And unpredictably as wind alters them
I hang on the whim
Of a certain girl
Who makes the kind of decision light makes in April.

WISH

I wish I could show you like waking Adam
A world of flower, of bird and tree
    Where each stream sang its name
Every beast printed its story :
There would be fields butterflies patterned
And there, jewel and dress, from a wood
Kingfishers would fly to your hand
    In words I remembered from childhood;
But the garden has to be made of rain
Across steel, brick, drooping coalsmoke :
    No easy beauty,
    Only the locked sea
    Pockmarked here in a dock,
And an asphalt pavement rainbow-flowered with oilstain.

WINTER NIGHT

You can hardly see through the window :
Jungles of frost have crusted the panes,
And winter night as we draw the curtains
Is settling on sheets of snow.
We lie wide awake then, talking of childhood,
While you remember some story
You would tell when you had no fire or food,
And your childhood frailty pierces me.
Love now is slow as snow in air :
A mediterranean vision —
Sea, flute, light — is gone;
Tonight, settling through time together,
Is the future a child imagined
And the past that, perhaps, will live in a woman's mind.

ENTRANCE TO A LANE

A man came

tasting

silence like water
water like silence

silence tasting like water
water like tasting silence

and

at the end

well water

well

silence.

GENERATIONS

Love girls still half in childhood like in sleep
Their hair eyelids that droop
To hide the sleeper's waking dream from siren
Telephone and the ironed
Light that the cleaners leave on streets.
                                                                      Men move
Impetuously through this girl's dream : their cars
Humiliate her father; their guitars
Have no question and answer; and her eyes
Are open to a light without surprise.

Film-gong sun clangs our hours out,
                                                            our
                                                                  hours.

FIVE IMAGES

When suddenly in April for an hour
The silken sky blows clear of all but birds
And light precision-cuts across the air
Unsteady traceries of leaves and buds;
When high across the houses rain dissolves,
Sky finds related blue – street-tar, roof-slate –
And colours all washed clearer than themselves
Bind into one intensity of light;
These five still unrelated images
Hint at what life could be : the springtime world
Laid open bare of cloud to any eyes,
Families here and there where love has held
A girl with painter's eyes, and her love-making,
And old man – clear, wise, vivid, and still working.

RHYME

Words are two a penny
Songs there are not many
Suns there are not any
But
One
And its god Apollo
By whom all divining
Is love singing
Gave me in his shining
Some-one that I follow
Like a winter swallow
Pointing with its winging
Cold
↓
Sun

VOICE

And always when this voice asks to be answered
It speaks in a dying wind : wind on a moor
Trundling an edge of rain like an old newspaper
Or wind in the head, blowing the past back
Fresh as rain on the face, in the birch-bark moonlight
Or the first wind of dawn when all things shrink
To a filing system for caging a smaller future.
What violence would I do by going back ?
What violence do I do, not going back ?